100 Day Healing Campaign

"Militantly Possessing Healing through Strategies of Prayer"

100 Day Healing Campaign

"Militantly Possessing Healing through Strategies of Prayer"

Copyright © 2020 by Rashaun Worley

Contact Author at: rashaunworley@gmail.com

ISBN Number: 978-1-7322286-1-0

Cover Photo Images: "Betibup33/Shutterstock.com"
Photo for the Back of the Book: Grycaj/Shutterstock.com
Cover Design From: Jamar Scott

Definitions From:
Strong, James. 2001. **Strong's exhaustive concordance** of the Bible. Abingdon Press

<u>*Dedication*</u>

This book of prayers is dedicated to the first love of my life, my mother. She was the epitome of an intercessor who taught me much of what I know to be true this day. Mommy, although you never saw the fulness of this work I am grateful that you were able to read it in its beginning stages and that you were pleased. As you dwell in the presence of the Lord forever, know that all that you have instilled in me and your mantle that now rests upon me as a man of prayer will not go without bearing much fruit for the Master. Secondly, to my wife Lynnea Worley: Thank you for your guidance through the process of birthing this work for the Master and loving and protecting me as I literally live out what is written in the pages to come. I love you.

Preface

This book is not about simply reading and reciting prayers, but a curriculum that leads the reader into the presence of the Lord. As you matriculate through its pages over the next 100 days, not only will you be challenged in your faith, but you will find yourself encountering Jesus in ways that you have never known before. Take this journey ready to not only be healed in your body, but also in your mind and spirit.

Table of Contents

Introduction

It is indeed the will of God that we be healed. It is written in His word. He has given us the remedy through for total wholeness. And He does not desire that we go through suffering. Jesus did the suffering on our behalf. Therefore, if we are yet striving with an illness or any bondage from the enemy, it is illegal. I believe that by the Spirit of God, I have come up with this campaign. As I was sitting in the infusion center waiting to have the port in my chest flushed, I began to think, *"What if I sought the Lord for healing for the next 100 days? What would be the results of seeking Him and believing His word for healing during this time? What would I learn about God as The Healer? How will this transform me in other areas other than my health?"* And so we begin.

This book contains a study of scriptures that I felt Holy Spirit guided me to concerning healing and what brings about healing. I wrote them and allowed revelation to uncover how they tie into God's perfect plan for us to be healed. Each day in the book has a scripture tied to it along with commentary and a prayer. Today is April 17, 2017 and I am beginning my journey of 100 days of healing.

The Reverential Fear of the Lord brings Healing

Day 1

"But to those who fear My Name the Sun of Righteousness shall arise with healing in His wings; and you shall go out and grow fat like stall-fed calves." **Malachi 4:2**

One key to healing is reverencing the Name of the Lord. When we reverence Him, it allows for Him to step into the midst of your suffering and overshadow all that burdens you. Rapha is the name of the Lord our Healer. Honor that name. Reverence it.

Prayer: Father, I honor you today. And I thank You because You are the Healer. It is indeed your will to heal us. So today, I submit to Your will. I come into alignment in my heart and my spirit with Your will. I say to You, your will be done in my life today. I reverence Your name as Jehovah Rapha, the Lord who heals, and I honor that so that the character of the Lord's name as healer, will be made manifest in my life. I am apart of the people who are called by Your name. And I come under the submission of who You are as healer. So arise, Healing God, with healing in Your wings! Release your healing now, In Jesus' name. Amen

Day 2

"Do not be wise in your own eyes; Fear the Lord and depart from evil. It will be health to your flesh and strength to your bones." **Proverbs 3:7-8**

When we worship the Lord, He will oftentimes give us instruction as to how to care for the thing that ails us or even His healing virtue may break forth in time spent in His presence. We should always seek the Lord's point of view concerning all matters and never think ourselves wise enough to do anything without Him.

Prayer: Father, your word says that we should trust in you with all of our hearts and lean not unto our own understanding. So today, I am willfully submitting my trust to you. I relinquish all rights to follow my own will and mind and take on the mind of Christ. Your word says to not be wise in my own eyes and to fear You and worship You! That it may bring health to my flesh and strength to my bones. As I worship you, Father, let strength come to me now and let health be restored to all my flesh. I thank you for doing this for me, in Jesus' name. Amen

God made a promise to the children of Israel in the desert, that if they would listen to His voice and reverence Him, that He would keep them whole and without sickness and disease that they knew in Egypt. That promise still stands today. For those of us who revere the Lord, He will heal us from any and every sickness and disease. It is in fact His heart and His will. In the next prayer, I have included a time of repentance as well as prayer for healing. Repentance is healthy and a blessing provided by the Lord for us to re-align ourselves with His will. Therefore, making us and keeping us eligible for all that He has for us in His will.

Day 3

"and said, "if you diligently heed the voice of the Lord your God and do what is right in His sight, give ear to His commandments and keep all His statues, I will put none of the diseases on you which I have brought on the Egyptians. For I am the Lord who heals you." **Exodus 15:26**

Prayer: Lord, I see now that worship keeps me safe. It allows me to dwell in Your presence as one dwells in a tent. Thank you for the promise that you would always protect me and keep me safe as my heart stays reverent towards You. I have a promise according to Your word in Exodus 15:26 that You would cause every foreign disease to my body and foreign to those who worship You, to bow to Your holy Name. I turn away from every way that is not like You. I am repentant of every deed and thought that does not line up with Your word. And so I reposition my heart to bow to Your will and way. You are Jehovah Rapha, the Lord who heals me. I receive Your healing now, In Jesus' name. Amen

Take time to go through previous scriptures on reverence and healing and meditate on them before going to next section.

Acknowledging the Healer

To acknowledge is to accept or admit the existence or truth of.

Day 4

One of the most important things to settle in our hearts as we continue to arrive at healing is to recognize Who in fact is the source of healing. Let it be cemented in the foremost parts of our being that God Himself is our healer. Not the antibiotics, the insulin, antiviral, or even antiretroviral. No, not even the chemotherapies, cocktails, or radiations. But it is God and God alone who holds all power to heal. And it is in deed His will and His heart that we be healed and made whole. No matter how grim the situation. He is the focus of our faith. Hebrews 11:6 says *"Without faith it is impossible to please Him, for he who comes to God must first believe that He is, and that He is a rewarder of those who diligently seek Him."* We must believe that He is what we need of Him to be in the time that we are seeking and that He will reward. God is the healing that we need. He will reward us healing as we diligently seek Him. When the children of Israel grieved the Lord and He sent serpents into the camp to vex them (Numbers 21), the Lord instructed Moses to take a bronze serpent and place it on a pole. Whoever looked up to the pole if bitten, would be healed. Jesus likened himself to the serpent lifted up in the desert by Moses in John 3:14. That whosoever would believe on the Lord Jesus would not perish but have eternal life. By Jesus being lifted up on the cross, He purchased our right to healing. He is our healing.

Prayer: Lord Jesus, I give You praise! I thank you for Your grace. I acknowledge you as my Healer. You bought my right to healing by being lifted up on the cross. When the serpents of sickness and disease came and injected their venoms into my flesh, I was not without hope. I can look up to You, even as the children of Israel looked upon the serpent that Moses held, and I know that I will be made whole. You are the Lord who heals me. I receive Your healing now by faith, In Jesus' name. Amen.

Day 5

I am reminded of the story of Naaman who was commander of the army of the king of Aram. Naaman had leprosy. His wife's servant, who was from Israel, suggested that Naaman go to see the prophet who lived in Samaria. She made the bold statement without waver that if he indeed sought out the prophet in Samaria that he would be cured of his leprosy (2 Kings 5). As we of course follow the story, Naaman goes to see Elisha who was in Samaria, bathes 7 times in the Jordan and is made whole according to the word of the Lord in Elisha. Naaman sought after the prophet of the Lord because a daughter of Israel acknowledged that her God was a healer. She firmly believed it. And boldly she declared it.

I believe that God honors our bold declarations of truth in who He is. This is the faith He seeks from us and will show up every time. Jeremiah claimed "is there no balm in Gilead?" (Jeremiah 8:22). Let our faith arise to make such bold confessions and acknowledge that indeed the Lord is our healer.

Prayer: Father, I bless You! You are faithful to your word and you hasten to your word to perform it. I acknowledge today in this very moment, as a son, that You are the balm in Gilead! It is you who causes our health to recover. I thank You for your healing balm now. And even as you were with the prophet Elisha who was sought after by the army commander, I thank you even now that Holy Spirit is here with me ready to perform the word of the Lord over my life that I may be healed. I receive Your healing now and I give you praise. In Jesus' name, Amen.

Healing by His Word

The word of the Lord is forever established in Heaven.
(Psalm 119:89)

His desire has always been a Kingdom legislature here on earth so that it reflects the laws and atmosphere of Heaven. When the Lord speaks a thing, He means it and never withdraws it. Everything He says is yes and amen. This is further reassurance that healing is absolutely His will and character. There is no sickness in Heaven and it is never sent from or mandated by God. As we know by now, His word is filled with promises of healing of the natural and spiritual bodies. This gives us great confidence in Him that if we search out and trust in Him, it will be unto us according to His amazing word.

Day 6

"My son, give attention to my words; Incline your ear to my sayings. Do not let them depart from your eyes; Keep them in the midst of your heart; For they are life to those who find them, and health to all their flesh." (**Proverbs 4:20-22**)

Prayer: Father, I thank you that you provided the remedy before there was ever an issue. You established everything I would need in heaven and give me access as a son to those resources. So I thank You that You have provided Your very word of life that provides healing and wholeness for me in every way! Holy Spirit, bring them back to the forefront of my heart and thoughts daily so that I may meditate on them and speak them over myself until they are embodied and made real in my life. I thank you Father, that you love me this much to see to it that Your perfect will is done in my life! This indeed is healing. In Jesus' name, Amen.

Day 7

"He sent His word and healed them, and delivered them from their destructions." (**Psalms 107:20**)

Prayer: Father, thank You for the life raft that you tossed out to me when I was in waters that were over my head. These waters of calamity, waters of infirmity, waters of affliction you are more than capable to deliver me out of them! I thank You, God for the word that you sent down from Heaven to heal me and deliver me from my destruction. You did not leave me abandoned. You harkened to my cry and delivered me. I receive the word you have sent that is echoing through out all creation declaring "Be Healed." I receive it now by faith, in Jesus' name. Amen.

It is imperative to take daily doses of His word and not miss a day as if you were on a strict medical regimen. It is the consistent meditation and repetition of this living word that will begin to take life form in your very body. It will cause your faith to rise and manifest God's very best for you. It's all by His design.

The Lord told Joshua that he should meditate on this book of the law and not cease neither day nor night and make sure to honor all that is in it. Then his way would be prosperous, and he would have good success. (Joshua 1:8) These scriptures should be on the forefront of our minds and hearts and in our mouths continuously confessing them as confession of what we believe until it comes to pass. This is the heritage of the children of God and His will concerning us.

Worship that Restores

Throughout scripture we can see instances that God answered to the needs of His people through their worship. As we worship the Lord, we are focused on everything that He is and nothing about what or who we are. We magnify, or make big, everything about Him that makes Him God and minimize any focus on us. Worship is a lifeline to our Life's Source. It connects us to His presence to access all that we need to continue to exist with purpose in the earth. Including the healing that we need for our physical bodies.

Day 8

"Bless the Lord, O my soul; And all that is within me, bless His holy name! Bless the Lord, O my soul, and forget not all His benefits: Who forgives all your iniquities, Who heals all your diseases...(**Psalm 103:1-3**)

Prayer: Father I bless You and give Your name praise. I honor You because you alone are God. You are holy, transcendently other than everything that I am. I reverence you. You are the One who forgives all of my iniquities and heals all of my diseases. Let this worship arise to You, Father and let Your healing stream flow to me. Restore me even now in Your presence. My soul blesses You, God. I love You. In Jesus' name, Amen.

Day 9

"Taste and see that the Lord is good; blessed is the man who trusts in Him! Oh, fear the Lord, you His saints! There is no want to those who fear Him. The young lions lack and suffer hunger; But those who seek the Lord shall not lack any good thing." (**Psalm 34:8-10**)

Prayer: I declare, Oh Lord, with my whole heart that You are good! No matter the circumstance, You are good! Although there may be much lack and famine around me, I can trust in You that You will provide for me! I am connected to my source! You are the source of my life and strength. Your word declares that if I trust in You, that I will not want for anything. This is including my healing. To seek You, Father is to have all that I need. I trust that You are faithful to Your word. I will worship and honor You forever. In Jesus' name, Amen.

Day 10

Day 10 reflections and Faith Assessment

Every 10th day, it is good to do a reflection, review and assessment of faith growth. I would say, if you sense your faith has not grown to believe God after the 10 days even a little, then do not continue and go back and repeat the first 10 days.

This should not be read as a book, but be read as meditations and mastication on the word of God. To deplete, if it were possible, all of the nutrients from these scriptures until there is nothing left and they literally overwhelm you with hope and confidence in the God who heals! Let this day be a day to rest and meditate on what He has been saying thus far and let Him strengthen you in mind, body and spirit.

"Finally, brethren, whatever things are true, whatever things are noble, whatever things are just, whatever things are pure, whatever things are lovely, whatever things are of good report, if there is any virtue and if there is anything praiseworthy-meditate on these things." (**Philippians 4:8**)

Prayer: Father I bless You. Your loving kindness is better than life. I thank You for this day and the opportunity to bask in Your awesome presence. Today Lord, I reflect back on what You have provided for me. Your words of healing, which are a sure foundation for me, will never fail. You are the God who can do anything but fail. Thank you for your great love and great grace that hovers over me even now. I ask that You will cause the words that I have meditated upon to run deep and cause strong roots to grow. Let them bring forth the desired fruit in its season. I honor You and value Your presence during this time of reflection and assessment. In Jesus' name, Amen.

Properly Responding to Fear

During this time of devotion and meditation, fear is the one enemy that will be sure to rear its ugly head. It will launch multiple accusations and arguments in order to get you to doubt, and break agreement with what God is saying concerning your situation. The Lord showed me that fear acts as a contractor and hit man in demon gangs. Its job is to bind you up and impede your progress so that the strongman can come in and complete its intent and will in your life. In this case, that strong man would be the spirit of death.

I believe it was very intentional of Holy Spirit to lead me to deal with fear on day 11. I researched the significance of 11 in scripture and found that it means "Disorder and Incompleteness." Fear wants to bring disorder and confusion to your focus so that you will not complete what God has given you to do. For me, so far in this process I have encountered different levels of this fear. Just 2 days ago, I had a doctor's appointment and the things I heard were not very delightful. In fact, they were slightly discouraging. Fear told me to turn my back on God because He would not fulfill His promises. It even suggested (although I did not listen) that I should consider suicide. It was then that Father began to speak and say, "Do not turn your back on me. Don't give up on me. I will make good on my promises. I cannot lie." And the peace of the Lord came with His words and began to comfort me. This is why it's very important to stay prayerful and worshipful beyond these daily meditations so that you can hear His voice in the darkest of times. After all, this is a warfare tactic against the enemy of sickness and infirmity.

One thing to keep in mind going into the next couple of days dispelling and exposing fear is this: The enemy fears that God WILL in fact fulfill His promises over you. And that fear actually EXCEEDS the fear that you have that God will not make good on His promises. Even your adversary has faith in God. Don't let him out do you.

Day 11

"For God has not given us a spirit of fear, but of power and of love and of a sound mind." (**2Timothy 1:7**)

The Hebraic word for fear is "yaw-ray". And one of the meanings in the original language is the psychological response to terror. Ref: Strongs Exhaustive Concordance. This is why the Lord emphasizes that He has given us His spirit that will bring about sanity and peace of mind.

Prayer: Father, I honor You today. You are good and perfect in all of Your ways. Everything about You exudes your perfect love towards us. For that, I give you praise. Father, when believing Your word, we have an adversary who comes to bring up lies and accusations in order to get us to doubt and be afraid. Father I am grateful that You are proactive and never reactive! You have said in your word that You have not given us a spirit of fear, but of power, love and a sound mind. I thank You, Jesus that your word stands true and cuts through every lie. Let this word be a shield of faith for me that will quench every lie thrown by the enemy. Protect my mind and my heart, Father as I continue this journey toward healing. Let everything around me speak of Your goodness and Your absolute intent to make healing my reality. In Jesus' name, Amen.

Day 12

One of the greatest and most affective tactics of fear is to make you feel alone. Your adversary knows that if he can make you feel alone, then he can amplify himself and give the illusion that he is bigger than your God. Once again, it's all a lie. Remember, that even when you don't feel Him, Holy Spirit is always there. He is just a call away and He is absolutely ready to respond.

"Yea, though I walk through the valley of the shadow of death, I will fear no evil; For You are with me; Your rod and Your staff, they comfort me." **(Psalms 23:4)**

Prayer: Father, I thank You that in Your word you said that You would never leave me nor forsake me. You are with me, even until the end of time. So when I feel like I am all alone and being overwhelmed, Father I thank You that you are near to me all the more. I need not be afraid. You are well equipped for whatever my enemy brings. You go to battle on my behalf. You are always armed with rod and staff to protect me as The Great Shepherd. I honor You, Lord Jesus. I pray, Holy Spirit, that You would release peace to my mind and silence every voice that speaks contrary to Your word. In times that I am most vulnerable, let Your voice ring the loudest and most familiar in the crowd! That I may know Your voice as your sheep, and not follow the voice of the deceiver. I make your Name bigger than fear! In Jesus' name, Amen.

Day 13

"The Lord is my light and my salvation; Whom shall I fear? The Lord is the strength of my life; Of whom shall I be afraid?" (**Psalm 27:1**)

Prayer: Father, I thank you that you are the one who turns on the lights to every secret operation of the enemy. The tactics used by hell to try to pressure me to give in to doubt and fear. I thank You, Father that you light my way and You alone are my salvation. You will always come to my rescue because I am Yours. Strengthen me, Oh God, that I may rise up with valor and courage to face this dark thing knowing that greater is He that is in me, than He that is in the world. Therefore, I will not fear! I give Your name glory now for the victory. In Jesus' name, Amen.

Day 14

It is the love of God that calms us and silences our fears. At times when we feel the most afraid, we should sit in His presence and simply receive His love. His love reassures us and gives us courage and confidence to proceed.

"There is no fear in love; but perfect love casts out fear, because fear involves torment. But he who fears has not been made perfect in love." (**1 John 4:18**)

Prayer: Father, I honor You. You are the source of my strength. You strengthen me and undergird me with Your great love. And because of Your love operating in me, I shall not fear. I thank You, Father, that you are canceling out every fear and apprehension to proceed forward. You are perfecting me in Your love day by day which drives out fear. And you are strengthening me and building me up with the courage and confidence I need. You are cementing in me my identity as one who is greatly loved by You. I receive Your love today. Let it be radiant in my countenance and evident in my walk. In Jesus' name, Amen.

After writing these scriptures and meditating on them as well as reading the prayers, I am learning that the biggest defense against fear is acknowledging to Whom You belong. Because I am His, I do not have to be afraid. He gives me all things to cause me to be equipped. His Spirit, His Love, and

His right hand of power are all I need to be strong and courageous. When fear surfaces again, simply remember that you belong to Him. You are His beloved.

Knowing Your Position

If you haven't figured it out by now, much of this process is indeed warfare. As we just finished the last section on fear, it was essential so that you can fight for freedom with clarity and focus. But now that we are not afraid and we are consistently being perfected in love, we need to know how we are positioned. One of the key things to position is a name. I remember at the time the Lord delivered me from a multiplicity of things, He began to speak to me and declare my name in the Heavens. The name that I "knew not of" that He had given me from long ago. I believe that this name holds in it, like a capsule, everything that defines my identity and purpose in Him. In it is everything that I am assigned to do, as a son of God in the earth. He began to declare that over me in order to break and reverse the characteristics and the names hell had given me.

When given a name, it begins to take on a character and becomes a living thing. For example, God calls us more than conquerors, warriors, deliverers, kings and priests who rule and reign. Whereas, the enemy will call us losers, unable to accomplish anything, adulterers, fornicators, homosexuals, etc. Anything that you can imagine that are not like God. Holy Spirit reminded me of how the Chaldeans changed the names of the Hebrew boys Hananiah, Mishael and Azariah. (Daniel 3) These names mean, "Yahweh is grace," "One who is asked for (or sought out)," "God helps". They were changed to "Servant of sin to god of the moon (Shadrach), "Who is what aku is (Meshach)," and "Servant of Nebo, god of wisdom (Abednego)." All of which were contrary to the true God they served. The tactics of hell are still active today. He wants to change your name. Once you begin to answer to these names, then your character will follow to conform to that which you are being called. That's why it is imperative to know what our Father has called and continue to speak over us this day.

Day 15

Prayer: Father, I give Your name glory. To Your name alone, all praise is due. I thank You, Father that it is in You that I find my identity. You give me a name that resounds throughout all creation and you set me in princely and kingly positions of authority. I ask, Lord that You would solidify in me the name that You have spoken over me that will drown out the prophesying of the enemy and his attempts to give me a name contrary to Your words. I cancel out every negative thing and word curse that Satan has tried to make stick to my life and destiny. And I declare that I am Yours and only what You have spoken concerning me is true. I am an overcomer through Christ who loves me. I am more than a conqueror. I will win and have already won! Even this battle, is a done deal because I am a son! In Jesus' name, Amen.

Day 16

"Behold, I give you the authority to trample on serpents and scorpions, and over all the power of the enemy, and nothing shall by any means hurt you." (**Luke 10:19**)

This scripture indeed does speak of our positioning and authority that is given to us through Jesus Christ our Lord. Therefore, we must trust the Lord's word that NOTHING BY ANY MEANS can hurt us.

Prayer: Lord Jesus, I thank You for the authority that You made available to me over my enemy. Because you overcame, you have made me an overcomer. You made a promise that nothing by any means will hurt me. So, I thank you that the current situation that I am in has no power over me. It must break and release its grip because it has been stripped of its power by Your blood! I thank you, Lord that (Insert disease, infirmity, bondage of any kind) has no power over me! As you have been delegated power from the Father, so have You delegated power unto us who are in You. I thank You Jesus for my freedom and power to tread upon the head of the serpents and scorpions through Your great triumph. In Jesus' name, Amen.

Day 17

We wage our warfare in the Kingdom from a seated position. The lure of the enemy is to get us to respond and remove ourselves from our seat of authority. Hell cannot remove you from authority, they can only try and get you to remove yourself. The best way to win this battle is to remain seated. Symptoms may arise, bad reports, accusations and persecutions from the enemy and more! Nevertheless, recognize them as a ploy and yet remain seated. You are above them all. They shall remain under foot.

"and raised us up together, and made us sit together in the heavenly places in Christ Jesus,..." (**Ephesians 2:6**)

Prayer: Father, I give your name glory today! You have caused me to be seated together with Jesus in the heavenlies. As I remain in Christ, I indeed hold my position of authority as it was given to me. And it is in this place that I wage all of my warfare. Father, I thank you for the grace to continue to remain seated no matter the situation or the circumstance. Through trial in body and mind, I thank You for strengthening my inner man to be able to keep my bearings through this intense attack. Break every distraction and silence every voice that is contrary to Yours and that would seek to lure me out of my seat of authority. I thank You, Lord for strength and wisdom during this time and the promise from You that I already have the victory. This battle is indeed already won through Christ. All honor to Your name.   In Jesus' name, Amen.

   *I would also like to note as I was doing some research after this prayer that the number 17 signifies biblically "Overcoming the enemy" or "Complete victory". I bless the God of Heaven for this revelation!

Day 18

I want to consider positioning also a place where we dwell. Psalms 91:1 says, *"He who dwells in the secret place of the Most High shall abide under the shadow of the Almighty."* And just like the seat of authority, there are great benefits of simply dwelling in the presence of God. I look at it this way, if it can't stand in His presence, then it can't harm me. Or, if it cannot survive His presence, then it can't stay on me. So even when it comes to sickness or any bondage, pressing and then remaining in the Presence of the Lord is a sure fire way to cause whatever it is to lose its grip. Although I could go on in just this one Psalm that is so full of great promises, I will return later and focus on another scripture with the same theme of dwelling for now. This scripture can be found in Isaiah.

"And the inhabitant will not say, "I am sick"; The people who dwell in it will be forgiven their iniquity." (**Isaiah 33:24**)

Prayer: Father I honor Your presence. I thank You that You have made for me a hiding place and a dwelling place in Your presence. And there, just as a baby in the womb of his mother, I find all things that I need. In You, I have security, nourishment and healing. Father, I thank You that there is safety from everything that seeks to harm me in Your dwelling place and as an inhabitant there I shall not say that I am sick. And every assignment from hell loses its grip because of the Oil of Your presence. I command every sickness, disease and infirmity to loose your hold in Jesus' name. I strip you of all authority and power and deem you illegal. I dwell in the Presence of the God who heals. Even whose name is Rapha. Father, I give You glory and honor. In Jesus' name, Amen.

Day 19

"Because you have made the Lord, who is my refuge, Even the Most High, your dwelling place, No evil shall befall you, nor shall any plague come near your dwelling;" (**Psalms 91:9,10**)

Prayer: Father, I thank You for Your promise that because I have made You my dwelling place, that no evil shall befall me, nor shall any plague come near my dwelling. You are my dwelling place and I hide myself and rest in You. I am refreshed in You. Continue to renew me, restore me and heal me in the place of Your presence as I yield all the more to Your Spirit. In Jesus' name, Amen.

Day 20 reflections and assessment

I was listening and asking the Lord what should I meditate on for the 20th day of the campaign. I wasn't sure if I should stay on position or begin to transition into 7 days of Thanksgiving and Fasting. Yes, Fasting. But I was quickly reminded that it was a 10th day and a day for reflection and assessment. Biblically, the number 20 signifies perfect or complete waiting. Waiting is indeed a position and we should always keep our minds and heart in position to wait upon the Lord. Not in a sense that we are inactive, but when we are waiting upon the Lord we are very active. We are meditating upon His promises and following the steps He gives us towards the realization of those promises. So for day 20, let's reflect on continuing to remove the fear and remembering our positions of authority, dwelling and waiting.

Day 20

"But those who wait on the Lord shall renew their strength; They shall mount up with wings like eagles, they shall run and not be weary, they shall walk and not faint." (**Isaiah 40:31**)

Prayer: Father, I bless You and honor You. I am grateful that You are removing every fear and doubt. You are stretching out on the inside of me and causing me to remove the barriers of my faith in You. I thank You that You have challenged and confronted my fears and doubts and began to settle within my heart my position in You. As a son, I do not have to fear. As a son, I am victorious in Christ. I am seated in High Authority because of Jesus and given access to come into and dwell in Your presence. Father, continue to teach me what it is to wait upon You so that my strength is renewed like the eagles and that the hope of every promise spoken over me will not fade but remain strong unto the day of fruition. I glorify the awesome name above every name! In the name of Jesus I pray, Amen.

7 Days of Thanksgiving and Fasting

For the next 7 days, I wanted to focus on giving thanks to the Lord for what He has done as a way to not over obsess on healing and forget that He has done so much even through this process. Thanksgiving is a good way to recalibrate and make sure that no seed of idolatry is planted and can take root. Keeping the Lord in proper perspective is very key in this campaign for healing. And I believe that thanksgiving moves God to "Do it again" so to speak, those things He has done before in your life and the lives of those around you. Fasting destroys bondages, reset focus, renews strength to fight, bring clarity and fans the flame in you for the Lord.

As we journey through scriptures of thanksgiving, reflect on one thing the Lord has done for you personally and give Him thanks and let this time be done with fasting. I do recommend consulting with your doctor and instruction from the Lord on how to fast. Which one is right for you?

Day 21

"Enter into His gates with thanksgiving, and into His courts with praise. Be thankful to Him, and bless His name." (**Psalms 100:4**)

Prayer 1: Father, I honor You. I thank You for this day. I thank You for the way that You have displayed Your love toward me this very day. The way that you have displayed how You are involved in every intricate detail of my life. Nothing is hidden from You. Most importantly, I am grateful that You have given me the key to your gate and the entry point into Your courts. And that way is thanksgiving and praise! So I praise You today, Lord that I may spend this day and the rest of my life with You in Your courts! Entering into Your gates with thanksgiving in my heart and into your courts with praise in my mouth! So I praised you! I bless You! In Jesus' name, Amen.

"I will praise You, O Lord, with my whole heart; I will tell of all your marvelous works. I will sing praise to Your name, O Most High. " (**Psalms 9:1-2**)

Prayer 2: Father, today I come asking for nothing. But today, I give You thanks. I set my heart to praise You for Your goodness. For the awesome things You have done on my behalf and the behalf of those around me. Lord, if I were to try and focus on all of Your goodness, indeed it would be overwhelming because You are just that good! So I lift my voice to You, and take my key with all creation and say thank You, Father! With my whole heart I praise You and give You thanks! With my whole heart I reflect on all of your marvelous works! Let my heart be reminded constantly of Your goodness when other things vie for my affections and attention. Let me return to the place and position of thanksgiving unto You, always. In Jesus' name, Amen.

Day 22

"Because Your loving-kindness is better than life, my lips shall praise You. Thus, I will bless You while I live; I will lift up my hands in Your name." (**Psalms 63:3-4**)

Prayer: Father, I give you glory today! I come acknowledging that You are good! You are greatly to be praised! Today I thank You for your compassions. I thank you God, for your loving kindness that is better than life. You are moved with loving kindness to act on our behalf. You acknowledge our low estate and Your heart is moved for us. Father, I ask that You would build in me, compassion for my neighbors and compassion for Your people. Let it be that when they are in need or they are hurting or lacking that the compassion of Jehovah arises in me! Let my heart be moved by what moves You. Father, let me not be consumed within myself or viewing others through a lens of self -righteousness and religion. Let me view through the lens of a heart full of loving-kindness. In Jesus' name I pray, Amen.

Mid-Fast week Nugget

Praise causes our disposition to change and lifts our countenances. Father never intends for us to look like what we are going through. Praise is our beauty as saints of God and takes our mind away from everything set to weigh us down. Praise is the heart gleaming in gratitude towards the Lord for

His mighty acts and wondrous works! In God's word, we are often admonished to wear praise as a garment. It brightens our very being as we stare into the face of the Son. Let us continue to give thanks unto the Lord as it renews our hope in Him and restores our joy.

Day 23

"Rejoice in the Lord, O you righteous! For praise from the upright is beautiful." **(Psalms 33:1)**

Prayer: Father, I bless You. I thank You that You have provided a mechanism whereby I can remain strong and keep my countenance while You fight on my behalf. I thank You that as I praise You Father, You cause Your light to shine upon me and it brings warmth and new perspective where there was coldness and gloom. Thank You, Jesus that You place a garment of praise on me that beautifies me and identifies me as one of Your own. Let praise never cease from my lips. Let it continuously be in my mouth. In Jesus' name, Amen.

Day 24

"Let us come before His presence with thanksgiving; Let us shout joyfully to Him with psalms." (**Psalms 95:2**)

Prayer: Father, I bless You! I come before Your presence with thanksgiving. I thank You, Father for this day. I thank You for Your great love toward me and Your mercy that has been bestowed upon me. Despite whatever is going on, because I am even praying this prayer is testament of Your goodness and Your faithfulness toward me. The very thing that wanted to take my life has not succeeded and I am able to give Your name glory and praise. Let praise erupt from me like a fountain! And place a new song of thanksgiving upon my lips that I may sing it with joy! I declare You are good, Father! I love You with my whole heart! Let my life honor You today and always. In Jesus' name, Amen.

The Lord increases those who give thanks all the more so that the voice of their thankfulness will not be diminished! What a beautiful sound it must be to Him. How He must enjoy when His children are thankful and outwardly appreciative of His goodness! Increase the sound of thankfulness in the ears of the Lord and prepare for great increase! It is day 25 of our journey. I am excited about this day because 25 means grace upon grace! Let us give thanks to the Lord for His abundance of grace!

Day 25

"Then out of them shall proceed thanksgiving and the voice of those who make merry; I will multiply them, and they shall not diminish; I will also glorify them, and they shall not be small." (**Jeremiah 30:19**)

Prayer: Father, I thank You today! I give You honor and my heart is overwhelmed with thanksgiving unto You. I am so ever thankful for Your grace. It is so undeserved, yet You bestow it upon us so bountifully. I thank You, Father that it is Your desire and Your good pleasure to bless us with Your grace. Even to give us grace upon grace. So Lord, let my heart be exuberant with praise unto You! Let it overflow with thanksgiving! For indeed according to Your word, you cause those who give thanksgiving to You to be great and not small! You allow your glory to rest upon them with thankful hearts! I love You Lord and I thank You for a new sound of thanksgiving proceeding from my heart! I take You at Your word and now receive grace and increase because of thanksgiving! In Jesus' name, Amen.

Day 26

"Oh give thanks unto the Lord, for He is good! For His mercy endures forever!" (**Psalms 107:1**)

Prayer: Thank You, Lord for Your goodness! Thank You, Lord for Your mercy that endures forever! Even when I am unfaithful to You, Your love supersedes my ability to remain consistent and true. Thank You, Perfect God that Your mercy and Your love is not contingent upon my ability to do everything right. Neither is it contingent upon how much I love You back. But You, Father loved me first and therefore I love You! You provide mercy unto those who cry out to You with pure heart intent. I honor You today, God. And with all my heart, I give You thanks! I love You, Lord. Let me continue to remember that You are good! And Your mercy endures forever! In Jesus' name, Amen.

The Love of God

A couple of days ago while we were still on the days of Thanksgiving, the Lord began to point out some things to me concerning my view of Him and understanding of His Love. I believe that we often are content with a head- knowledge and very eloquent and wordy explanation of God's Love without ever really knowing and experiencing that Love for ourselves. I am going to be a little bold and even say that it is kind of impossible to really know God without having experienced His Love. We cannot know Him without having a deep revelation in our hearts, spirit, and mind of His unfailing and great Love. So, I began to create a language in prayer that would open up the conversation between God and I about His love. What does that look like? What does that feel like? How can I experience it? How can I know it? Let's see what scripture has to say for the next few days about the Love of God. For the first day, let's practice praying a prayer that Paul prayed for the Ephesians.

Day 27

"…that Christ may dwell in your hearts through faith; that you, being rooted and grounded in love, may be able to comprehend with all the saints what is the width and length and depth and height—to know the love of Christ which passes knowledge; that you may be filled with all the fullness of God." (**Ephesians 3:17-19**)

Prayer: Father, I bless You and honor You. I thank You today for Your great love toward us. This love was first placed on open display by how You gave Your Son, Jesus for our sins. And this very same love motivated Him to die for our freedom from every manner of bondage. Now Father, I ask that You would reveal this love in a deeper way. That I may begin to understand Your love, beyond my understanding and know it beyond my knowing. Give me an experience with Your love that will mark and transform my life forever. I want to know You, Father. I want to love You more than ever before. So, show me Your love, God that I may love, honor and worship You in the way that You require. In Jesus' name, Amen.

If we do not have a proper understanding and knowing of God's love, we can easily become guilty of simply "working to earn" what the Father gives us freely. As I am writing this, I have felt as if I have hit a brick wall in flow. But I am beginning to think that this wall is intentional on

God's part. I sense that He is changing my total perspective on things and that He wants me to see that in His love, He has provided all that I would ever need and the equipment for whatever I will do for Him. It's not something I can work for, but it is something that I have to train myself to open up to receive and experience as it does not come naturally for us. We have to be intentional in our yielding to His love daily in order to receive. Through faith, He dwells in our hearts and causes us to be rooted and grounded in His love and gives us the ability to comprehend it. I believe this should be the foundation to all things in the Christian life. From His love flows every gift and ever provision is hidden in it. Selah

Day 28

"But God, who is rich in mercy, because of His great love with which He loved us…" (**Ephesians 2:4**)

Prayer: Father tonight I honor You. I thank You for Your presence here and Your readiness to display Your love. I ask You Father, that You would help me to open up to receive Your love. The love that You are consistently pouring out, but my human mind cannot perceive. Give me a deeper understanding of Your great love with which You have loved me. And help me to see, Great Father that it is in this love that I have everything that I need. In the name of Jesus I pray, Amen.

Day 29

"He who did not spare His own Son, but delivered Him up for us all, how shall He not with Him also freely give us all things?" (**Romans 8:32**)

Prayer: Father I thank You! I thank You for a love that has no limit. And every day that I live, Your plan is to reveal this love to me and to not keep it hidden from me. You desire to love me extravagantly. The same extravagant love that You showed when You gave up Your own Son just for me and freely give me all things as You have given Him. I bless You, God. Help this to become more and more my reality daily as I seek out Your love and your heart. Help me to be endowed in this extravagant love so that through me, others may come to know Your love that frees, Your love that conquers, And Your love that provides. In Jesus' name, Amen.

Day 30 Soak and reflect on last 10 days

Here we are at the ending of another 10-day period. Mixed with times of Thanksgiving and Fasting and transitioning into The Love of God. I would take this devotional time to combine the two. First, begin to give Him thanks for all things and then thanks for how He loves us. Then, invite Holy Spirit to come and express His love in whatever way He sees fit. Receive this love and then reciprocate it in whichever way you feel moved to do so. Let this be the beginning or the continuation of an intimate mode of daily communication and reaction to your Heavenly Father. He wishes to know you in this intimate way.

Day 30

"Who shall separate us from the love of Christ? Shall tribulation, or distress, or persecution, or famine, or nakedness, or peril, or sword?" (**Roman 8:35**)

Prayer: Father, I honor You. Thank You for Your goodness toward me. Thank You for Your mercy toward me. I bless You Father for all that You have done in my life and will continue to do. I thank You, Father for Your great love that You have displayed and continue to display before me. And in this great love, You have provided all things that I will ever need. Father, I am grateful for Your love that protects and keeps me. Yes, this Your love that stayed on a cross and took stripes to heal me. Lord Jesus, I thank You that You made a promise in Your word that nothing has the power of authority to separate me from Your great love. Help me to remember this even when times are hard, that You are ever with me Father. Help me to run to You in worship, never doubting that Your love for me is unfailing. And when tribulation and persecution from my enemies seem overwhelming, cover me in Your love and let me give thanks to You that You have already overcome every enemy I would ever face. I thank You, Father that because of Your love, I am more than a conqueror and that even this I will overcome! Your love is unfailing and never ending! I give You all glory and Honor! It belongs to Your name alone. In Jesus' name, Amen.

Strength Renewal

It is the beginning of the second leg of the journey. We are here on day 31 of this campaign for healing. The Lord has been good and shown Himself true and faithful. It is not to be unexpected that of course our adversary would seek to thwart, distract and distort so that we would take our eyes off of the end prize of this journey. As a reminder of why we started, it is because we absolutely believe God for healing in every stubborn, unyielding, and even aggressive area of our lives. I believe that there will be one testimony and it will be without a "but" clause. It will be a completed work and there will be no "except" clause. So, with that in mind let's rebuild and regroup with a fresh wind and renewed strength! This battle is a strong one and for many, may even have been a long one. That's why we depend on the strength of the Lord to endure. *His strength is made perfect in our weakness.* (2 Corinthians 12:9) Let us set our heart and mind on the Lord who is the One who gives and replenishes our strength to fight. We expect the strength of the Lord to rise up in us and carry us all the way through.

Day 31

"And He said to me, "My grace is sufficient for you, for My strength is made perfect in weakness." Therefore most gladly I will rather boast in my infirmities, that the power of Christ may rest upon me." (**2 Corinthians 12:9**)

Prayer: Father, I thank You for your grace. The grace that is sufficient for me. The grace that allows Your strength to be made perfect in my weakness. I thank You, Lord that as I plow through this journey that I am not alone. And that in every place that I grow weary, there You are to replenish me. There You are to cause Your power to rest upon me. I thank You, Father that knowing this battle would be greater than me, You had already made provisions of strength for me through Your grace. Therefore, I can boast and be glad because Your power will show up in my life. So I renounce weariness. I renounce fear. I renounce intimidation. I receive from the reservoirs of Your love, a renewed strength! I receive Your peace to my heart and mind. I pronounce my decision to move forward. In Jesus' name, Amen.

Day 32

"that He would grant you, according to the riches of His glory, to be strengthened with might through His Spirit in the inner man..." **(Ephesians 3:16)**

Prayer: Father I honor You today. I thank You for Your unfailing love and Your great heart towards me. Thank You for grace and mercy that keeps me every day. That keeps me protected from every trap and snare. I thank You, Father that You strengthen me even according to the riches of Your glory. I thank You, Holy Spirit that as You prove stronger and stronger in me that I am strengthened in my inner man with might. I yield to You today, that You may prove to be the very source of my inner strength. Thank You, for breathing strength into me by the working of Your great power according to the riches of Your glorious presence in me. And I pray as I continue along this journey and every path that You would set before me, that I will continue to grow in Your might and in Your power, Father. For without it, I can do nothing as it is in You that I move, live and have my very being. So, I acknowledge that all of my help comes from You. I thank You, Lord for this even now and receive Your strength in me. In Jesus' name, Amen.

Day 33

"Then he said to them, "Go your way, eat the fat, drink the sweet, and send portions to those for whom nothing was prepared; for this day is holy to our Lord. Do not sorrow, for the joy of the Lord is your strength." (**Nehemiah 8:10**)

As we are waiting for our healing to manifest physically, we continue on our perspective journeys and mandates that we have obtained from the Lord. We keep ourselves busy attending to the work of the Lord. We are speaking His word to others. We are praying for the healing of others. And if you see their healing manifest, as I have many times, and not your own; don't be sorrowful in this! Know that the Lord is faithful! His promises are sure. They are yes, and amen. And what He has done for them, will He not do the same for you? We rejoice when others receive their blessings because we know that if we have sown prayers of healing into the lives of others, the Lord will not forget that. I believe God honors what you sow and causes it to bring back a harvest for you in the season of your life that you need it most! So let your heart be at peace! The time is near and even is now for your healing!

Prayer: Lord, I thank You today. I thank You for your joy in me that is my strength! You admonished us through Your servant, Nehemiah that we should go ahead and continue to live Kingdom lives for Your glory. That we should go forth not sulking or lying in a bed of self-pity, for Your joy is our strength. It will keep us until the full manifestation of Your promise arrives! So I honor You, Lord that Your joy carries me when I grow weary. It renews my strength. And even now, Your joy is giving me the strength that I need to endure along the path of righteousness to bring me into a place of rest from battle and a harvest of healing. I give You glory for this. In Jesus' name, Amen.

Day 34

"Finally, my brethren, be strong in the Lord and in the power of His might." (**Ephesians 6:10**)

Prayer: Lord, thank You making me strong in You. Thank You, Father that You are strengthening me with might, by Your Spirit, in my inner man. You are giving me the ability to push through and persevere in this fight and in my assignment. I honor You, Father as the very source of my strength and it is You, Holy Spirit that causes me to excel. I pray, Father that You would continue to build me up even like an edifice as I continue to press into You. In Jesus' name, Amen.

The Anointing

The anointing of the Lord is His Spirit of power that comes upon a person in order to do a job that cannot be accomplished in their natural ability. Jesus Christ (The anointed One) was indeed God in the flesh. However, His temple of flesh limited Him as it limits us. So, He needed the anointing in order to do everything that He was sent to do. Jesus did not do anything in His 33 years of life before Holy Spirit rested upon Him after the baptism by John. After that, it is then He left for a season of fasting and then went into ministry. With Jesus as our model, we too need God's anointing upon us in order to do the impossible. For in ourselves, we can do nothing. But with God, all things are possible! In this session, we will focus on the anointing of God. What do the scriptures say about it and how do we pray and ask for it.

Day 35

"The Spirit of the Lord God is upon Me, because the Lord has anointed Me to preach good tidings to the poor; He has sent Me to heal the brokenhearted, to proclaim liberty to the captives, and the opening of the prisons to those who are bound…" **(Isaiah 61)**

Prayer: Father, I thank You that You have made a way for us to be able to do the impossible. Through Your Son Jesus, we now have access to a power that is greater than our own. I thank You, Lord for the anointing that rests upon me so that I can be free according to Your word in Isaiah. I ask now, Father that Your anointing rests upon me, and break the back of the spirit of infirmity that has attached itself to my life. I pray, Lord that Your anointing would fall upon me from Heaven and even smash every demonic entity on my life and on the lives of those in close proximity to me. Thank You, God that because of the anointing that I can proclaim freedom and liberty to captives as I formally was captive. I thank You and receive Your anointing now. In Jesus' name, Amen.

Growing up in church, I have always heard the saying "The anointing destroys the yoke." This is very true and can be backed up scripturally. God intends for us to completely rely on His power. It's what any good parent would want for their children. He doesn't desire that we would be lacking in anything or fighting any battle on our own. His anointing is available to heal.

Day 36

"It shall come to pass in that day that his burden will be taken away from your shoulder, and his yoke from your neck, and the yoke will be destroyed because of the anointing oil."
(Isaiah 10:27)

Prayer: Father, thank You for grace and power. Thank You for the oil that destroys the yoke! Even Your anointing upon us! Thank You, Father that it is Your will that we be set free from every burden and bondage of the enemy! And that You break the yoke from around our necks so that we are never again enslaved by hell and its tactics. I honor You and give You praise. In Jesus' name, Amen.

Day 37

"But we have this treasure in earthen vessels, that the excellence of the power may be of God and not of us." (**2 Corinthians 4:7**)

Prayer: God of power, I thank You that You rule and You reign. I give You glory and ascribe honor and strength to You. Father, I honor You because of Your power that causes me to break forth and break through every barrier and every obstacle set before me. This power is Your Holy Spirit in me. It indeed is a treasure within me and an utter display of Your excellent power. I thank You, that because of Your power in me I am victorious over every circumstance! I victor even now, over sickness and infirmity! I declare freedom now, in Jesus' name. Amen.

Day 38

"Is anyone among you sick? Let him call for the elders of the church, and let them pray over him, anointing him with oil in the name of the Lord." (**James 5:14**)

Prayer: Father, thank You for the oil that saves the sick and raises them up from the bed of their affliction. You, Great Holy Spirit, have made accessible this oil from the reservoirs of Heaven just for us, to raise us up and make us well again. As I anoint myself with oil today, I pray with great faith that Your will is made manifest in my physical body. I declare complete healing over me now in Jesus' name. I speak peace to every ailing area in my body, mind and spirit. And I declare that the Kingdom of God reigns over my life. In Jesus' name, amen.

Day 39

"You prepare a table before me in the presence of my enemies; you anoint my head with oil; my cup runs over." **(Psalm 23:5)**

Prayer: Father, I honor You. Thank You for the oil that refreshes me! You anoint my head with oil when I grow weary and tired as the Good Shepherd. When the harshness of life beats down on me, You cover me, Holy Spirit like an ointment on a fresh wound. I thank You for resting on me and keeping in dire times. I ask that you would continue to pour out fresh oil for this battle I must fight! I thank You, that I will be too oily for the enemy to keep a good grip and that they will witness with front row seating the mighty hand and favor of the Lord in my life. I give You glory and praise for this. In Jesus' name, Amen.

Day 40 Reflection, Assessment and Prayer

As I reflect upon the last 10 days, I know one thing is for sure; the heat has been turned up on me from the enemy. If this is you too, just know that greater is He who is in us than he who is in the world. We can do this. So, as we reflect on strength and anointing, I am reminded of Samson. He had the strength of the Lord and was God's anointed deliverer for the nation of Israel. The only thing the enemy could do was to bring him into a place of lost focus and deception in order to cause him to fall and lose strength and the anointing to lift. Although we are in modern day, the tactics of hell are still pretty much the same. We will stand our guard. We will keep our posts and we will settle our position in Him. He will cause us to triumph because of His great strength and because of the anointing.

Day 40

Prayer: Great God, the One who all power belongs to. The One who sits upon Majesty in the Heavens. Creator, the One who set the worlds into formation and orbit by the power of His word. I bless You and acknowledge You as Lord above all. You are God above all gods and there is absolutely no one like You. Father today, I ask that You continue to strengthen me. Build me up solidly, oh God so that there are no loose ends within me. Strengthen me to my very core that I may be able to stand in this battle! I am completely dependent upon Your grace that is sufficient and Your strength that is made perfect in my weakness. I thank You, Father that You are pouring out in new measure the oil of Your anointing for the assignment at hand. It is the anointing that will destroy every yoke of bondage and lift the heavy burden. Help me to continue to stay focused on You and lead me into a life of complete discipline by Your Spirit, so that my mind has no room to wonder. I thank You for this now and I give You all glory and honor. In Jesus' name, amen.

Soaking in the Presence of the Lord

Just as one would have a bath daily, it is just as important to soak in the presence of the Lord. What does it mean to soak in His presence? It is the intentional waiting and sitting in the presence of the Lord. Allowing Him to pour His love upon You like a shower. In soaking, we gain confidence, our faith is increased and strength is imparted among other things. We are cleansed. We are sanctified and peace overcomes us like a river. The Lord will also speak to our situations and speak life into our world of turmoil as we soak or abide with intent in His presence.

Life can cause us to want to rush away and become busy, but our Father longs for us to "sit for a spell" as they would say in the Deep South and spend some quality time with Him. How do we do this affectively? By His word and His spirit! Let's look at some scriptures of meditation and let's intentionally initiate engaging His presence and soaking there for a few days. Turn on some worship music or sing a song to the Lord from your heart and invite Him to come.

Day 41

"This Book of the Law shall not depart from your mouth, but you shall meditate in it day and night, that you may observe to do according to all that is written in it. For then you will make your way prosperous, and then you will have good success." (**Joshua 1:8**)

Prayer: I come to You now, Father. Meet me where I am. I honor You. I adore Your name. I desire Your presence here. I welcome You here now. I make way for You to enter in and do as You please. You are worthy to be worshipped and adored. As Your presence enters in, Father speak to me, wash over me and make me new. You make all things new. As I meditate upon Your word, open the eyes of my understanding and let there be illuminating revelation so that I may see You all the more. Thank You for Your presence here. In Jesus' name, Amen. *Soak and wait for the Lord*

Day 42

"But his delight is in the law of the Lord, And in His law he meditates day and night." (**Psalms 1:2**)

Prayer: Father, I honor You today. I thank You that You have given Your written word for us to meditate upon that will lead us to Your presence. Show me what it is to meditate upon Your word and to glean on every syllable. So that I can know You as I have never known You before. So that I can experience Your love and grace in a new way each day. I thank You, Lord for this act of freedom You have set for us through meditating on Your word. Grant grace unto me to search for Your heart all the more and abide in Your presence through my meditation. In Jesus' name, Amen.

One of the greatest benefits of sitting and soaking in the presence of God is being able to inquire of Him and He speaks to you. All of the answers to all of your questions can be found in His presence. We never have to guess about God, we can always know His will. All we have to do is ask.

Day 43

"One thing I have desired of the Lord, that will I seek: That I may dwell in the house of the Lord all the days of my life, to behold the beauty of the Lord, and to inquire in His temple."
(Psalms 27:4)

Prayer: I honor Your presence, Father. Thank You for Your great love for me that provides access to Your presence. Having the heart of a Father, You never desire for me to wander around hopeless or void of understanding as You give all things freely. Thank You, Father that in Your presence I can find everything that I need. Healing, direction, strength, freedom and joy are all found in Your presence. I ask that this would be my portion for the remainder of my life, to abide in Your presence daily and inquire of You as my source and as the spirit of Wisdom that guides my life's course. I bless You and praise You now. In Jesus' name, Amen.

Day 44

"In the year that King Uzziah died, I saw the Lord sitting on a throne, high and lifted up, and the train of His robe filled the temple." **(Isaiah 6:1)**

The Lord's presence will cause us to see and have understanding of purpose and vision. It will bring healing to our broken identities and speak to our purpose and destiny, which causes us to overcome in every area. Including sickness. So then, sitting with the Lord on a daily basis will strengthen you in understanding your "reason" and your "why" behind your existence so that the enemies against your life have no right to stay any longer.

Prayer: Father, I honor You today. I thank You for Your kindness towards me. I thank You for Your love that is unfailing. I ask today that Your presence would fill this space where I am as it did in the day Isaiah's eyes were opened. Open my eyes to see You, Father in a new and spectacular way. Let Your presence bring clarity to my being and existence which empowers me to overcome. I yield now, Holy Spirit so that You may have Your way and begin to speak over me and define my future which does not include sickness of any sort. I thank You that Your very presence cancels the prognosis of the enemy and ensures me that I will walk in complete wholeness. I thank You now and give Your name glory and praise. In Jesus' name I pray, Amen.

Day 45

"But from there you will seek the Lord your God, and you will find Him if you seek Him with all your heart and all your soul." (**Deuteronomy 4:29**)

Prayer: Lord, I thank You that You gave a promise that if I would seek You with all my heart and all my soul that I would find You. This was not a conditional, but something that was certain. I thank You for the reassurance that You are near to those who call upon You. You hover over us by Your Spirit. I ask You today Lord that You would reveal Yourself to me in a new way as I seek You. Let your presence permeate through my very being. I welcome You here now. In Jesus' name, Amen.

Day 46

Today during my prayer time, I began to reposition my heart to give God thanks for the things He had already done and provided. I spent time giving God glory and praise. I sensed that as I did that, not only was it what the Lord was asking for in that moment but also what needed to happen as I felt that it unlocked provisions that were held back from me. Although we are seeking the Lord for the manifestation of His promises, we must always turn back to say thanks and ascribe unto Him glory that is already due to Him. This also draws His presence near to us and a thankful heart will keep Him close to us.

"Give unto the Lord the glory due to His name; worship the Lord in the beauty of holiness." (**Psalms 29:2**)

Prayer: Father I bless You! I give You all of the glory and praise because it belongs to You! All praises are due unto Your name. Today, I set my heart aright to thank You for all that You have already done! Thank You, God that You have risen from Your place of rest as Jehovah Jireh! You are the Lord who has provided and provides and have positioned provisions for the future. I love You, Lord. Let a spirit of praise and thanksgiving rest upon me that I may forever give Your name glory and that praise would exude from my very being. And let Your presence rest over me as I give honor to Your name. In Jesus' name, Amen.

Day 47

"You will show me the path of life; In Your presence is fullness of joy; at Your right hand are pleasures forevermore." (**Psalms 16:11**)

Prayer: Lord I honor You. I thank You for Your presence. In Your presence is the fullness of joy. My joy is restored in the place of Your presence. My joy is renewed in Your presence and You begin to show me the path of life that I may have freedom and liberty! Lord, allow me to experience Your presence like never before. I give you full permission to the doorway to my world that You may come in at will. Father, help me to honor Your presence and treat you rightly that I may not offend Your precious Holy Spirit. Thank You that there are pleasures for me at Your right hand. Thank You that You are beginning to unfold Your hand to me that I may be satisfied. I give Your name glory and honor. In Jesus' name, Amen.

Day 48

The freedom that comes from being in the presence of the Lord is unmatched. No matter what has you down, the presence of the Lord will bring freedom and liberty. It is guaranteed. Meditate on that fact that it is indeed a guarantee and not a maybe. Whatever it is that ails you, or is plaguing you. Whatever weight and sin that is clinging to you like slime, be cleansed and let it be released in the presence of the Lord. With a repentant heart, go before His presence sincerely.

"Now the Lord is the Spirit; and where the Spirit of the Lord is, there is liberty." (**II Corinthians 3:17**)

Prayer: Lord, only Your presence can set me at liberty. In this world, there are so many weights and sins that easily beset us. I ask that Your presence come now and relieve me of these burdens. Your yoke is easy and Your burden is light. Lord Jesus, I ask Your forgiveness of these things that weigh me down and reveal any other hidden thing in me that is not like You. For Your presence alone I live. Let my life honor You. In Jesus' name, Amen.

Day 49

"You shall hide them in the secret place of Your presence from the plots of man; You shall keep them secretly in a pavilion from the strife of tongues." (**Psalm 31:20**)

Prayer: Father, I thank You for hiding me in the secret place of Your presence. Your presence for me is a fortress where I am safe from all the plans and plots of my enemies. In times of despair, cause me to always run towards Your presence and never the devices of my own heart for they are deceitful! In Your presence is made known the way of life! I honor You for that Father. Thank You for the ability to access the place of Your presence through Jesus Christ, my Lord. I give You glory, and honor and praise. In Jesus' name, Amen.

Day 50 for reflection, prayer and meditation

Here we are at the halfway point of our journey! I pray that you feel the Lord doing something in you beyond the physical. It is what is done in your spirit man that is going to be the cause of overcoming every infirmity and disease in the body. Proverbs 18:14 states "The spirit of a man will sustain him in sickness, but who can bear a broken spirit?" When the Lord begins a healing work, I believe it happens from the inside out. What is the point of having a body that is whole when the spirit is broken? At this halfway point be encouraged and know that no matter what you see that may not be different, and no matter what the adversary has thrown at you during this time; you will indeed win! The victory is yours and God is doing an amazing work in you. Continue to trust Him. Let us continue through worship, through prayer and fasting, through combating fear, acknowledging the need for the anointing, through praise and thanksgiving and through soaking in His presence to grab hold of what is our inherent right as children of royalty.

Day 50

Prayer: Father, I bless You today. I thank You for what You have done thus far and what You will continue to do in and through me as I continue along this journey. In this moment, Father I make an altar unto You as my way of saying

"Yes" to continuing in Your way along this journey of healing. Break what You desire to break in me and build what You desire to build. Father, let me experience Your breaking and building presence along the next 50 days that will produce the person that is renewed and made whole that I desire to see. I give all of the glory to You. In Jesus' name, Amen.

Power Belongs to God

When going through a storm, everything wants to vie for your faith. The statistics have their testimonies. The doctor declares, "Trust my diagnosis, because I have the degree." The pharmacist says, "You can't live without this medicine." The researcher says, " There is no cure for your situation." All the while, the Lord is asking, "Would you like to know what I have to say?" All of these things are no match for our God! When chances are slim and things are grim is when He does His best work. Rest assured, that God indeed has the final say! **Power belongs to God**. He is the Omnipotent One! Jesus declared upon His resurrection, "All power is given unto me in Heaven and Earth." (Matthew 28:18) It doesn't matter a hill of beans what anything or anyone else has to say, if power rests in His hands then it rests on me! He has His hand upon me! And nothing can take me out of His hand!

Day 51

"God has spoken once, Twice have I heard this: That power belongs to God." (**Psalm 62:11**)

Prayer: Father, I honor You and ascribe to You great strength! All of creation reverberates that power belongs to You, Oh Great God. This power that causes the sea to never cross its borders and at the same time, keeps the Earth in her orbit. Let it resound through and through in me, Father that You alone have the power. Let it permeate my soul and surpass all of my human wisdom. Because of Your omnipotence, I am on the winning side. Because You have the power, nothing else has the authority to end my life or degrade its quality. I thank You for that. Now God, by the power that is in Your great name, I speak to this infirmity and this situation to be removed and cast into the sea. Never to be a hindrance to me again! Put Your power on display! In Jesus' might name, Amen.

Day 52

"Behold, I am the Lord, the God of all flesh. Is there anything too hard for Me?" (**Jeremiah 32:27**)

Prayer: I bless You, Oh God! All majesty and honor belongs to You. You are the creator of Heaven and Earth and all the power is Yours! So Lord, when things look scary and the enemy has boasted of himself a little more than he should have, remind me that You are the God of all flesh and that there is nothing too hard for You! You are not a God that is full of hot air and empty promises, but You declare only the things that You fully intend to make good on! I thank You, Father for Your faithfulness towards me and the assurance that You give me that Your words will be fulfilled, every one of them. I give you praise and thanks. In Jesus' name, amen.

Day 53

" For the Lord of hosts has purposed, and who will annul it? His hand is stretched out, and who will turn it back?" **(Isaiah 14:27)**

Prayer: Thank You, Father that nothing can impede the momentum of Your strength! You have purposed to do great and mighty acts on my behalf and nothing that I or anyone else could do can stop You. I thank You, Lord that Your hand is out stretched toward the enemies of my soul and the enemies of Your will and it will not be reversed! For You have declared that these enemies I will see no more because You are the Lord God almighty who fights on my behalf! I give You reverence, Great King. In Jesus' name, amen.

Day 54

"But we have this treasure in earthen vessels, so that the surpassing greatness of the power will be of God and not from ourselves." (**2 Corinthians 4:7**)

Prayer: Holy Spirit, I reverence You. I acknowledge that Your great power is at full force in me. And because of that, I know that all things will bow down to You. Thank You, Holy Spirit for Your power being harnessed in me like an atomic bomb. I ask now that it be released on my behalf against all sickness, disease and infirmity that has taken up illegal residence in my body. I declare that my body is the temple of the Holy Ghost! And for that reason, anything attacking my body, it will be destroyed! In Jesus' name, amen.

Day 55

"...And the power of the Lord was present to heal them." **(Luke 5:17)**

Prayer: Father, You declare in your word that You are a very present help in the time of trouble. (Psalm 46:1) I have no need to worry or to fear because you are with me. And with You being ever so present, so is Your power to heal. As I rest in Your presence now Father, consume in Your great power every manner of sickness and disease. Let it disintegrate upon initial contact with Your power. I ask now, that fire falls upon the head of the enemies of my physical body and for them to never be seen again! And I will declare Your greatness in the earth always! In the powerful name of Jesus, amen.

Day 56

"Let the groaning of the prisoner come before You; according to the greatness of Your power, preserve those who are appointed to die." (**Psalm 79:11**)

Prayer: Righteous God, it is in You that we have access to total freedom over every area of our lives. I praise You because it is Your perfect will that we be made free and whole from every entity that would have us bound. Oh Lord, I cry out to You as a prisoner to my infirmity and I ask that according to Your great power that You set me free. I thank You Father even now for preserving me by Your love and by Your Son's blood. In Jesus' name I claim total freedom and victory, Amen.

Day 57

"But if the Spirit of Him who raised Jesus from the dead dwells in you, He who raised Christ from the dead will also give life to your mortal bodies through His Spirit who dwells in you." (**Romans 8:11**)

Prayer: Father, it is stated in Your word that it is in You that we live and move and have our being. That is, that Your Holy Spirit dwells on the inside of us and feeds our very bodies the essence of life because of Your presence. Thank You Holy Spirit for quickening my body to bring life to what once was counted as dead. Because I have dedicated my body to You, You would not have Your temple be defiled by anything not like You. Sickness is not like You. So, I declare healing to my body now by the working of Your great power! The same power that raised Christ from the dead. Thank You for the healing now in Jesus' name, Amen.

Day 58

"Trust in the Lord forever, For in YAH, the Lord, is everlasting strength." (**Isaiah 26:4**)

Prayer: Father, I reverence You because all glory, and strength belongs to You. I thank You that Your strength is a sure foundation even as a rock that I can be confident in. You will not fail me. Thank You God that You will not fail me. Again, I say: Thank You Faithful Father that YOU WILL NOT FAIL ME. You are the God that will place His power on display on the behalf of those who love You and who cry out to You in great faith knowing that You will in deed show up. I will therefore trust in You and Your everlasting strength in the most Powerful Name of Jesus, Amen.

Day 59

"The Lord your God in your midst, The Mighty One, will save;..." (**Zephaniah 3:17**)

Prayer: You are indeed Mighty, Oh Lord. And there is no other power that is able to save. Arise in Your strength and in Your might on my behalf, Oh God. Save me from all that seeks to claim my life and trample underfoot every threat to my physical body. And I will give You all glory for unto You belong all power and glory forever! In Jesus' name, Amen.

Day 60

Day 60 Expressions of Worship and Prayer

It is the 60th day of the journey. If you have made it this far, give yourself a high five! Add a pat on the back as well! Encourage yourself and challenge yourself to believe God all the more for your healing! If I know the Lord, at whichever moment that your heart completely yielded to the truth of His word, is the moment that your healing came. In my heart I believe that for many of you reading this, it will not take until you complete this book for your healing to manifest. Some of you got it in the beginning. Some will receive in the middle and some may have to go until the end.

This book was designed to be a tactic of education, warfare and strategy to come to an ultimate goal. If you truly engaged your hearts and mind to the truth of God's word through out this campaign, I dare to believe that Jesus Himself has come into your world to prove Himself to be Healer and all that you will ever need and more. Let's use day 60 as a day of worshipful expressions and prayer. Let's show the Lord that we love Him because of His goodness and faithfulness towards us. Let's bow before our King who so bountifully bestows upon us all of His love and who keeps all of His promises. Lay before Him as He washes over you in His presence and continues to perfect the work that He has begun in you. Worship your God and King.

Day 61

Day 61 Let's Chat and Pray

Throughout God's word, there are promises of physical healing and health. From Deuteronomy all the way to the Psalms and beyond, the Lord echoes His heart concerning our well-being and prosperity in every area of our lives if we would simply trust and believe His word. These written nuggets of love are not all that God has said and in fact, He is still speaking today concerning the subject matter. Our God is the God who speaks! Our God is not mute, deaf or dumb. There is still Rhema that proceeds from the Throne Room of Heaven. God is still sending a word of healing (refer to Psalm 107 v20) to us today in our specific situations. Maybe you have perceived that a word just for you has dropped into your spirit that was inspired as you took this journey. What an amazing thing if this is true for you. Make sure to hold dear to that word and write it down. However, do not just write it down but cherish this word that the Lord has given you personally.

Oftentimes, we will take a word that we received from a prophet or even a word that was spoken directly to us by Holy Spirit and we are excited enough just to write it down. But then, we do nothing else with it. Maybe if you are diligent, you may have revisited this word a few times then sometimes forget about it. This is not the way that our Father desires that we treat His promises that He gives to us out of His heart. Think of it this way; say you are having a conversation with someone and you are pouring your heart out to him or her and telling him or her how you are going to purchase something for them because you adore them and they are excited in that moment. Then, as time goes by and you remind them of the promise that you made and they have a "yea, sure...ok" attitude concerning the situation. How would you feel? I know I would feel slightly offended and sad. I have been guilty in my own life of taking the words that the Lord speak and writing them down in little books all over the place but rarely revisiting them or praying those words. God wants us to cherish the promises that He gives us. When I heard this from the Lord, my first action of course was to have a repentant heart concerning the matter. Then, I needed to ask myself did I really know what it meant to cherish something. I mean, sure I had heard of the word because I've only been speaking English my entire life. But, what did the word cherish really mean and why would God use that word? Cherish defined in this context was: To keep a hope or ambition in one's mind. Another definition was to hold dear or to highly value.

I believe that when we cherish the words of our Good Father who loves us with an everlasting love, that it does something in the heavenlies. That promise receives an extra weight or push upon it to come to pass on our behalf. I believe that when we cherish the Word of the Lord that it employs those that excel in strength, our warring angels, to see that word all the way to manifestation in the earth. Cherishing will cause that word to come to fruition in our lives with expedition. With that in mind, we need new perspective on how to view the prophetic word. In times past, we have just taken them at a very surface value and then sit them on the table with all things common. Let us set our hearts to ask The Father for new perspective on how to view and cherish His promises.

Prayer: Father, I adore you. I adore the words that You speak because they are spirit and they are life. I ask that You would forgive me for times past where I treated Your words as those of mere men. Renew my heart so that I can see Your promises in a new way. That I would not just view them as a good word or an on time word, but a rightly word spoken in season with power to transform my very life even as quickly as that initial moment. Let me hold on to Your words as a life raft that You have thrown out to me in the midst of gravely deep waters. I want to cherish them, Father. And so let it be that the cherished word of the Lord on my life would not return to You void, but with the good report of accomplishment! In Jesus' name is my prayer, Amen.

Cherish His Promises

Day 62

"as His divine power has given to us all things that pertain to life and godliness, through the knowledge of Him who called us by glory and virtue, by which have been given to us exceedingly great and precious promises, that through these you may be partakers of the divine nature, having escaped the corruption that is in the world through lust." (**2 Peter 1:3-4**)

Prayer: Father, You have given us all things that pertain to life and godliness and included in that are great and precious promises. Just as the scripture has said, these promises are indeed precious. Encapsulated within them is everything I need to reach my highest potential in You. Holy Spirit, help me to hold every promise of the Father dear to my heart and highly regard them every day of my life until manifestation. In Christ's name I pray, Amen.

Day 63

" This charge I commit to you, son Timothy, according to the prophecies previously made concerning you, that by them you may wage the good warfare." (**1Tim 1:18**)

Prayer: Lord, cause me to hold on to Your word ever so tightly so that it may be used as a weapon against the enemy of fear and deception. Let Your word keep me alert and focused during this time. May the word that You have given me, Oh God be used as a two-edged sword in my hand that I may wage the good warfare and bring utter defeat to all things not like You. In Jesus' name, Amen.

Day 64

"He also taught me, and said to me: Let your heart retain my words; Keep my commands, and live." (**Proverbs 4:4**)

Prayer: Lord I honor You for Your goodness. I thank You that You are the One who teaches me in Your ways. You have desired that I would keep Your words and Your commands so that I would live. I say to You today, embed Your words into the deepest chambers of my heart so that I will cherish them. Let them spring forth from my heart like a summer rose to remind me of Your faithfulness and Your truth. Let them bring light to the dark places in my heart and cause life to flourish where there was death. I thank You for Your word that You have given me so that I may live. I cherish them always. In Jesus' name, Amen.

Day 65

"For the eyes of the Lord run to and fro throughout the whole earth , to show Himself strong on behalf of those whose heart is loyal to Him...." (**II Chronicles 16:9**)

Prayer: Father, You are the Lord God who is strong and mighty! Yes, the Lord who is mighty in battle. You are always alert and ready to show Yourself strong on the behalf of Your children. May my heart always be counted as loyal to You in trusting and keeping Your words, always. I honor You, Great King. In Jesus' name, Amen.

Day 66

"Your word I have hidden in my heart, That I might not sin against You." (**Psalms 119:11**)

Prayer: Father, I ask that You would engrave Your word permanently upon my heart that I may not turn to my left nor to my right but face straight ahead in trusting You. Let Your word be hidden in my heart, Father, to be a guiding compass through wildernesses, and a naval sextant in the rough seas of life to guide me all the way through to a safe place in You. As I cherish Your word, Oh God let Your peace keep my heart and mind until we've reached a safe landing. In Jesus' name, Amen.

Day 67

"I will meditate on Your precepts, and contemplate Your ways. I will delight myself in Your statues; I will not forget Your word." (**Psalms 119:15,16**)

Prayer: Lord, there are times that life gets really tough. And it seems as if there is no solid answer to any of its problems. Help me to remember Your word in these dark times. Cause it to be so that Your word is so engraved upon the tablets of my heart and seared into my conscience that it will be the first thing that comes to mind in every situation. Let a spirit of Holy Meditation come upon me that I will meditate upon Your ways and Your precepts always so that I may walk in the Light of Your Truth in the darkest of times. This is my prayer in Jesus' name, Amen.

Day 68

"My son, keep my words, and treasure my commands within you. Keep my commands and live, and my law as the apple of your eye." (**Proverbs 7:1,2**)

Prayer: Father, I make my vow to You that I will treasure and cherish your commands deep within my heart. I vow to You today, that I will keep them in the forefront of my thoughts and allow them to guide my actions. You have made a promise to me that if I keep Your commands that I will live. I believe Your word to be the assurance and the title deed to the things that I stand in need of. I honor and adore Your words concerning my life. Let them never depart from deep within me. In Jesus' name, Amen.

Day 69

"This Book of the Law shall not depart from your mouth, but you shall meditate in it day and night, that you may observe to do according to all that is written in it. For then you will make your way prosperous, and then you will have good success." (**Joshua 1:8**)

Prayer: Lord, I thank You that You promise to bring good success in my life as I forsake not to keep Your word ever before me. I thank You that Your word promises to make my way a prosperous one as I meditate day and night upon Your laws and precepts. I ask, Father, that You would extend grace to me that I might continuously keep Your word in my mouth always and never let them depart no matter the circumstance. For this I honor You and I give You praise, In Jesus' name, Amen.

30 Days of Intercession

10 Days for the Soul

In the last 69 days, we have done so much. And yet, there is much work to be done. You may have noticed that as much as this journey was concerning your healing, it also took some of that focus and placed it on Christ alone. This is what we should always do whenever a need arises. That is, not focus so much on our need but fine-tune our focus onto Him. I sincerely believe that God has caused your healing to arise like the morning sun. I believe that it is done! I will even dare to say that many of you received your healing before you ever made it to this point. To that I say, Congratulations! And to God be all the glory! However, I adjure you to press on until the final day. For the final 30 days, each day we will focus on praying for the need of someone else. It could be someone or no one in particular each day, but there is always the need for intercession. There is always a special blessing that is added to those who pray for the needs of someone else. It is one of the most profound principles in our faith and an earthly demonstration of the current ministry that Christ does for us every single day.

Isaiah 59:15-16 says "...Then the Lord saw it, and it displeased Him that there was no justice. He saw that there was no man and wondered that there was no intercessor..." Wherever there is a brother or sister who is suffering, it is at the hands of the devil. This is considered bondage and we must fight so that they can be free. No one should ever be left alone to fight on his or her own. Christ did not leave us alone and therefore we should not leave anyone else to fight alone. In other areas in the book of Isaiah, this is proven to be a theme of God's heart. We will look at many of the common things that people of all ages all over the world suffer with and begin to intercede for their freedom. As always, if Holy Spirit gives you more to pray for, please be obedient to Him. He always knows what to pray as He knows the perfect will and mind of the Father.

Let this time of intercession not be done as casual reading, but be postured in your heart as you read out loud and declare the freedom of your brothers and sisters all around the world. Just as Christ has set you free, let's petition and war for their freedom. These prayers are going to be general, but please call the name of the one/ones that Holy Spirit may show you as you pray these prayers! Remember that the effectual, fervent prayers of the righteous avail much! (Jam 5:16)

Day 70- **Depression**

Prayer: Father, we thank You today that in Your presence is the fullness of Joy. And because of the Body that was torn as the temple veil and Blood shed by Your dear Son, we have direct access into Your presence at all times. So now in Jesus' name, we pray that the Presence of the Lord would show up in the life of our brothers and sisters (or insert a name if you know one personally) who are being tormented with depression. We speak hope into every situation that has presented itself as hopeless to them and we take authority over ever whisper of despair from the evil one in their minds. In Jesus' name, we ask that You, Holy Spirit would be right where they are and surround them in Your overwhelming love. Cause Your love to drive out every fear and disparity and keep their minds in perfect peace as it shifts its focus to be stayed upon You. We release a peace that passes all understanding over them now and let them find sweet rest in Your presence. In Jesus' name, Amen.

Day 71- **Anxiety**

Prayer: Lord, You said in Your word to be anxious for nothing, but through prayer and supplication to let our requests be made known. (Phil 4:6) Yet, life can carry us to a place and we can hardly find our way back to You. So now, God of Peace, we ask that You bring our brothers and sisters who suffer from anxiety back from this place in Jesus' name. Cause every racing thought to cease even down to the molecular level. We speak calmness over them now and break the spirit of hysteria off of their lives. Let there be a release of refreshing and reassurance that what You have begun in their lives will be completed and that all of their needs will be and have been met in Christ the Lord. In His name we pray, Amen.

Day 72- **Anger**

Prayer: God, I thank that Your joy is our strength. And wherever Your presence is, there is the fullness of joy. So now Father, I pray that Your presence would envelop my brother/sister who is angry right now. Father, help them to release the anger that has lodged in their hearts and seeks to bring sabotage and destruction to their destiny and purpose. Open their eyes to see that the end of a thing is better than the beginning thereof and that there are brighter days ahead. I thank You now, Father that anger is no longer their portion but joyfulness of heart and perfect peace will take the place where anger once was. Let there be a joyful sound released from their bellies as You, Holy Spirit begin to fill them with Your joy! In Jesus' name, amen.

Day 73- **Grief**

Grief can be a very touchy subject. In no way is this to make light of the significance of losing a loved one. Grief, in itself is healthy and human. We grieve because we love. Jesus shows us this during His life as well. In my personal experience, one can experience a myriad of emotions during the onset of grief and perhaps throughout the process of healing. I do not have a soothing method for this or a plan to walk through it. What I could recommend is this: allow Holy Spirit to come into the intimate space of grief with you. He will counsel you, protect your heart and bring you back to a bright and healthy place again. He wants to be in the thick of it with you and bring you peace. You mean so much to Him and He loves you greatly. He is hurt when you are hurting. Remember, we do not have a High Priest who cannot sympathize with our weaknesses. (Heb 4:15) This includes grief and the heart ache it brings. So, this prayer will only be for a grief that the enemy wants to prolong in your life to bring you to a place of hopelessness and ultimately untimely death.

Prayer: Father, Your word says that You are near to the brokenhearted. (Psalm 34:18). So Father, I pray right now for my brother/sister whose heart has been broken by way of a loss. Grief has now settled in and has not allowed them to heal. It is Your will that they be healed even from prolonged grief. So in the name of Jesus, I pray that the bands of grief be broken. Let there be a release of the oil of Joy over them now and place upon them the garment of praise for the spirit of despair. Father, I thank you now that as grief is being broken off of their lives that healing is now taking place. I decree it to be so and not otherwise. In Jesus' name, amen.

Day 74- **Trauma (Prevents forward progression)**

Prayer: Father, in Your word it states that " the chastisement for our peace was upon You." So today I pray that the traumas that would cause my brother/sister to not walk in peace would be eradicated now in Jesus' name. Every shank of trauma that has been lodged into the soul of my brother/sister be removed now! I release healing in that place in Jesus' name. I declare that wholeness and forward progression will be their portion! And no longer shall they remain stagnated at the entry point of trauma in Jesus' name, Amen!

Day 75- **Un-forgiveness**

Where there is un-forgiveness, we can rest assured that there will be some manner of infirmity. Reason being is that un-forgiveness acts as a door holder to allow even stronger bands of wickedness, sickness and disease to come in. These unwanted guess, after so long a visit claim the right to be there and remain and gradually break down a man from the inside out. We must not allow un-forgiveness to remain not even for a day.

Prayer: Father, You said in Your word that if we do not forgive that neither would our Father in heaven forgive us. Lord, we know that forgiving can be difficult at times because of the pain we have endured. So, today I pray for my brother/sister who is struggling to forgive and it has caused them to be bound in their physical body. Let Your love penetrate the hardened walls of their heart and cause the poisons of un-forgiveness to be release. Help them to remember, Father, that there is great reward when we make the decision to forgive. Allow them to see that their healing is on the other-side of them making the decision to forgive. I thank You now for the healing that will be made manifest when they forgive. In Jesus' name, amen.

Day 76- **Resentment**

Prayer: Lord, I pray against the spirit of resentment that may reside on the inside of the heart of my brother/sister. Wherever they were wronged, Lord You are able to make it right again. Right every wrong on their behalf and cause their enemies to pay back one hundred fold everything that was taken illegally from them. With a heart full of praise and thanksgiving, I thank You now that because resentment is being evicted from the chambers of their heart that true healing will be their fruit. In Jesus' name, amen.

Day 77- **Betrayal**

Prayer: Thank You, Lord Jesus that You are a friend that sticks closer than a brother. I ask that You would be with my brother/sister now in their time of betrayal. Now more than ever, they need to feel the tangible reality of Your presence. I pray that You would heal their hearts from the sting of betrayal and remind them that You promised that You would never leave us nor forsake us. You are the bearer of all our secrets and the healer of all of our hurts. I thank You that after betrayal that we can live, love and trust again because of You. There is no friend like You and we honor You. It is in Your name that we pray, amen.

Day 78- **Abandonment**

Prayer: Lord, help us to understand that You are ever present with us. I pray today for my brother/sister who is feeling abandoned in this moment. Open the eyes of their realization that You are always with them. People will love and leave us constantly but Your love remains always. Your love knows no bounds and even if we make our bed in hell, Your love would find us there. Thank you, Lord Jesus that when others abandon us, You will take us in and we are never abandoned.

Day 79- **Injustice**

Prayer: Father, there are times where others have done us wrong or we were blamed for something unjustly. Because of it, we harbor anger and the feeling of injustice. But, You said that revenge is Yours and that You will repay. You are our Righteous Judge. You are the One who sees all and no amount of darkness can hide any wrongdoings. So, Father I pray for my brother/sister that You would right every wrong in their lives and heal them from the hurt of injustice. Cause there to be recompense for every wrongdoing and cause them to release all feelings of vengefulness over to You. You are the God that will repay! You are the God of recompense. Thank You, Father that You are the God of reset and making all things new. In Jesus' name we pray, Amen.

10 Days of Intercession for the Body

The final days of the campaign will be spent in intercession on ailments of the physical body specifically. It is my hope that as you have taken this journey with me, that our God has done something so miraculous and amazing in your life and body. Maybe He has even begun to speak to your heart concerning some additional prayer points of your own. Nevertheless, let this campaign be a tool that can be referred to at anytime on the behalf of yourself and others. I have tried to cover as many categories of disease as possible, but if the Lord brings anymore to the forefront of your heart as you pray, please address them.

Day 80- **Psychosomatic Disorder**

Psychosomatic Symptoms are defined as an illness or condition that is caused by mental stress or worry.

Prayer: Father, I thank You for grace and power over Psychosomatic Disorders through Christ's blood. Remind us when the enemy comes in with fear-filled words that You, Lord Jesus, have already won the victory for us. So, I speak peace to the mind and the heart and command the whispers of the spirit of fear to cease. I speak total peace from every false symptom caused by mental stress and fear now. In Jesus' name, Amen.

Day 81- **Cardiovascular Diseases**

Cardiovascular Diseases can be anything that attacks the heart to make it weak including damage to blood vessels or any structural damage to the heart that would cause it not to function the way it was created to function.

Prayer: Jehovah Rapha, I call on Your name today because You are healer of all diseases! I thank You, Father that there is victory in that name over cardiovascular disease. I speak over every function of the heart and command it to line up with the original purpose and intents of its creation. I thank You, Jesus that blood vessels and arteries are free from blockage and properly maneuvering blood flow to and from the heart in the way they were intended. I speak normal heartbeat with strength and vitality in Jesus' name. I command every murmur of the heart to cease. Irregular heartbeat, I command that there be normality and regularity to the heartbeat in Jesus' name. I thank You, Father that this is according to Your will and it is so. Amen.

Day 82- **Pulmonary Diseases and Disorders**

Pulmonary diseases and disorders are caused by anything that obstructs proper oxygen flow and makes it difficult to breathe. This is including but not limited to asthmas, degradation of pulmonary arteries and various allergies etc.

Prayer: Father, the most important thing that You ever gave us was Your Ruach (breath) so that we would become living souls. I thank You today and always for that. In gratitude and recognition that it is a privilege and not a right to even be able to breathe, I pray for my brothers and sisters who find it hard to do so on their own due to diseases and disorders of their pulmonary system. I speak to air passages to open thoroughly and completely for them. I speak strength to the lungs and even the muscles that support lung function in Jesus' name. I thank you, Father that there is now a new flow of oxygen to their bodies as You begin to breathe a fresh wind from Your very life-giving Spirit into them now. Holy Spirit, do what You have always done even from the beginning of time! Give them life and vitality in Jesus' name. Amen.

Day 83- **Autoimmune Illnesses and Diseases**

Autoimmune illnesses and diseases occur when the body attacks itself and breaks down its own defenses. For the most part, it can no longer recognize who is friend and who is foe. The list of different types of autoimmune diseases is quite a lengthy one. Nevertheless, the Blood of Jesus covers and conquers them all.

Prayer: Father, I pray for my brothers and sisters who suffer from autoimmune diseases. Those who suffer from lupus, arthritis of any kind, diabetes I or whatever the name of the disease may be (insert the name), it is subject unto the name of Jesus. I speak to their bodies now and command the confusion and inability to recognize its own allies to cease in Jesus' name. I thank You, Jesus that the self-created war of their bodies on its own immune system is now over! Let there be peace in their bodies so that they may in return glorify You! In Jesus' name I pray, Amen.

Day 84- **HIV/AIDS**

I strategically chose this disease to be the day after autoimmune illnesses and diseases because they are closely related. However, the issue is not that the body is attacking itself because of inability to recognize its own defense systems. In this case, there is in fact an outside force that has come into the body and has begun to break down the body's defenses from the inside out. The human immunodeficiency virus (HIV) prevents the body from fighting off things that may even be minute to others. If not treated properly or found too late, it will cause the body to go into a syndrome known as AIDS. At the stage of AIDS, the body is left completely vulnerable and incapable of protecting itself and ultimately falling to the demise of even the weakest of infections like the common cold.

Prayer: Holy Spirit, I honor You. I thank You, that You are the greatest Force in the Earth. And because of that fact, I thank You that You have authority even over HIV/AIDS. I pray on the behalf of my brothers and sisters who have been subjected to this monster of a disease. Let them know God, that it is in deed Your will that they be healed. And even now, I pray against the spirit of fear that their healing will not manifest. I release the power of the Holy Spirit against this wickedness now in Jesus' name and command fighter cells to regain their strength. I command the increase in T-Cells in their blood until it is restored to normalcy. I thank You, Father that the HIV virus is being rendered ineffective in Jesus' name and must exit their bodies. Thank You, Holy Spirit that the full legislation of the Kingdom is being released against HIV/AIDS now on the behalf of those You love. In Jesus' name, Amen.

Day 85- **Cancers**

Cancers form within the body when there are abnormal cells that rapidly duplicate and begin to kill and overtake healthy cells. Most often, they form solid tumors if they are within the tissues of the organs. However, if it is a blood related cancer, it normally does not form solid tumors. Nevertheless, whether blood related or otherwise, they are all subject to the Blood of Jesus Christ.

Prayer: Lord Jesus, You said in Your word that every knee will bow and every tongue will confess that You alone are Lord to the glory of God the Father. So, in the most powerful name in the Universe, I speak to cancer in the body of my brother/sister and I break your authoritative hold. I command total healing and restoration. Let there be a supernatural replenishing of healthy blood cells and tissue cells in Jesus' name. I speak a complete halt to metathesizing cells and command a reversal. Let healing be released and total restoration. Be healed of Breast Cancers, Lung Cancers, Liver Cancers, Stomach and Colon Cancers in the name of Jesus! Be healed of Leukemias and Lymphomas and Brain Cancers! Be made whole in Jesus' name! Amen.

Day 86- **Type II Diabetes**

Type II Diabetes is a disease that affects the way the body breaks down sugars. The pancreas in a healthy body makes enough insulin to break down sugar but this is not the case for one who may be diabetic causing them to need outside assistance. Also, this form of diabetes can be an inherited disease from a parent. Even then, it is not what God intended for us.

Prayer: Father, I pray for those who suffer from Type II Diabetes. I pray that while there are medical advances in this area, You would bring total healing to their bodies. Heal them in the place of their pancreas that they are able to metabolize the excess sugars in their bodies. I speak healing to the places where this disease may have affected them. I pray for soothing of nerve damage and pain and numbness of limbs. Thank You, Lord Jesus for the total restoration of their bodies. Amen.

Day 87- **Digestive Diseases and Disorders**

Digestive Diseases and Disorders are any malady that would cause one to not be able to properly digest and/or metabolize nutrients from food. This can include diseases like Celiac Disease, Irritable Bowel Syndrome, Crohn's Disease and many others.

Prayer: Lord Jesus, thank You that every disease is subject unto Your powerful name. You are our Great Physician and You are to be worshipped. I speak to the digestive disease that has taken up residence in the body of my brother/sister and I disarm it. This part of the body of the body was designed to bring us centering and provide nutrients to our natural bodies so that we can be empowered to expand the Kingdom of God in the earth. I command natural purpose be restored. Let every symptom cease and let there be absorption of nutrients and normal metabolism again. I evict every foreign invader and parasite in Jesus' name. I thank You Holy Spirit for Your light being released in the place of the digestive system now. Let healing be received in Jesus' name amen.

Day 88- **Nervous System Disorders**

When speaking of the nervous system disorders, it includes any and all diseases that deal with the sending and receiving of signals sent by the brain to all parts of the body. The nervous system is made up of your brain, spinal cord, sensory organs and the billions of nerves throughout the body that transport these signals.

Prayer: Father, I thank You for total healing and restoration from every nervous system disorder. I strip its authority to bring confusion and unrest to the body of my brother/sister. I command the cease and desist of every involuntary movement, muscular degeneration and loss of control of motor faculties now in Jesus' name. Thank You, Father that You are bringing peace to the storm that was nervous system disorder to their bodies now. We give Your name praise. Amen.

Day 89- **Mental Disorders**

Mental Disorders come in a variety of packages. Oftentimes, doctors have a hard time diagnosing a person with a mental disorder into one specific category as the symptoms may cross many lines. Essentially, a mental disorder is any of the conditions that would cause a person to not be able to think or make decisions clearly, have acute mood changes or inflict self- harm.

Prayer: Lord, Your word says in Isaiah 26:3 that You would keep our minds in perfect peace whose mind is stayed on You. This would be hard for the one who suffers from a mental disorder. So, in the name of Jesus, I break the power of darkness over the mind of my brother/sister. I speak the Lord's peace and light into their mind now. I silence every voice that speaks from hell to convince them that life is over and there is no reason to live. I silence every noise that would be bring distorted vision and thinking to them and I release the serenity of heaven into their minds. Thank You, Jesus that You have authority over the seen and the unseen worlds, even the worlds of our minds. Be enthroned in the mind of my brother/sister now and give them the mind that was also in You, in Jesus' name. Amen.

10 Days of Intercession for Personal Needs

Day 90- **Life Decision**

Prayer: Lord, I thank You for being the God who knows the beginning from the end. You have said in Your word that the steps of a righteous man are ordered by You so I thank You on the behalf of my brother/sister who is in the middle of making a life decision right now. I ask Father, that you would give them wisdom and insight into Your plans and Your will so that they would make the decision that is best for them and that is according to Your ultimate plan. Let there be provision for every need along this journey for them and let there be glory given unto Your name. In Jesus' name, amen.

Day 91- **Financial**

Prayer: Father, You are the giver of every good and perfect gift. You said in Your word that if we had a need for bread that You would not give us rocks instead. You would see to it that we have everything we needed. On the behalf of my brother/sister who is in financial need now I come to You. You are the Lord God who provides for us. I thank You now that everywhere there is lack you will cause there to be an overflow. Thank You, Father, for surprise gifts and even lost money found that will answer their needs. We honor You, God for being the God of more than enough and there is no bill, no bankruptcy, no unpaid debt or any other financial crisis that is too hard for You! Thanking You in advance in Jesus' name, amen.

Day 92- **Career/Job**

Prayer: Lord Jesus, You said in Your word that we should seek first the Kingdom of God and His righteousness and all other things would be added. (Matt 6:33) I thank You that this includes anything that we will need in order to seek out and progress the Kingdom here on Earth. This includes our Careers and Jobs. I thank You, Father, that even our Careers were written into Your plan for our lives. Thank You that You have the Career path for us that would go in congruence with how we are called according to Your purposes. I ask now on the behalf of my brother/sister that You would make that path clear and that You would guide them in the process of career choice and decision. Thank You, Father that the Career and Job that was purposed for them was simply awaiting their arrival. There are people and even angels set in place for them that are holding their spots on the job in eager expectation. I thank You for the favor that awaits them there in their set place. And in Jesus' name, I pray that it will manifest now so that there will be no lack in their storehouses and barns. All this I pray in Your Son's name, amen.

Day 93- **Business Decisions**

Prayer: Father, You have said in Your word that if we commit our plans to You, that You would establish our thoughts. (Proverbs 16:3). I pray for my brother/sister who is in the midst of making a business decision. I ask, Lord that Your will be made manifest in their lives. I pray that the odds would be in their favor and that every businessman/woman that has impure intent will be exposed. Thank You, God that You will cause there to be success on their behalf because they have placed You first and seek Your counsel. In Jesus' name, amen.

Day 94- **Finding Love**

Prayer: Father, You are the giver of every good and perfect gift! What a gift you gave us through the giving of Your only Son, Jesus! And this gift was given because of Your great love! So as I pray for my brother/sister to find love, I am reminded that love in itself is a gift. I pray that they would find this gift as they find themselves in You. And when the one that You have for them is revealed, let them be full of Your Spirit and grace to be the perfect helpmeet for their destinies. I thank You, Father for the husband who will love his wife as Christ loves the church and gave Himself for her. And for the wife who will submit herself and undergird her husband as the favor that the Lord has bestowed upon Him as he who finds a wife finds a good thing and obtains favor from the Lord (Prov 18:22). Thank You, God for helping these to find a love that was worth waiting for! In Jesus' name I pray this prayer, Amen.

Day 95- **Reconciliation of a Broken Marriage**

Prayer: Lord Jesus, no one knows better than You what it means to be apart of a broken relationship. For it has been said in Your word that You are married to the backslider. (Jer 3:14) Yet, You have reconciled us unto Yourself and given us the ministry of reconciliation. So I thank You, Father that even what may seem unrepairable and unsalvageable can be made whole by Your power and grace. I pray right now for my loved ones who are suffering a broken marriage. Ignite the fire of their love once again Lord. Let streams of the spirit of forgiveness and mercy begin to permeate their hearts and home as they communicate and boldly dare to love one another again. I thank You, Father that there will be peace in their home and I declare a cease fire concerning who was right and who was wrong and who did what. Marriage is a weapon against the tactics of hell and there is yet purpose in You bringing these two together and I speak the blessings and peace of God to rule and abide now in Jesus' name, amen.

Day 96- **Wayward Child/dren**

Prayer: Father, I pray for the child(dren) of my loved ones who have gone astray and live wayward lives. I pray that Your grace will find them where they are and lead them into the safety of the arms of Jesus. Cause them to realize that everything that they feel they lack is found in You. Their destiny is found in You. Their identity is found only in You. I pray, Father that You will reveal Yourself to them in a way they have never known and a way that they will never forget. Reveal Your glory to them so that they will forever be transformed and come into the knowledge of Your saving grace and love. In Jesus' name, Amen.

Day 97- **Unsaved Loved One**

Prayer: Lord, You said in Your word that it is Your will that none should perish, but that all would come to repentance. (2 Peter 3:9) I pray for our unsaved loved ones Lord that they would come into the knowledge of Your truth and love. Remove the scales from their eyes, Father so that the Light of Christ will begin to illuminate the dark places of their hearts and minds and bring them to repentance unto salvation. I thank You, Jesus that You provided the way for us back to the Father by Your blood and have given us the gift of salvation from ultimate destruction. I believe You for the salvation of my loved one that they will come into the fold of the beloved of God. Help them to find their way. These things I pray in Jesus' name, Amen.

Day 98- **Rededication to Christ**

If you or someone you know has gone awry and drifted away from God, be reminded that He has not drifted away from you! The Father is pleased with the very decision for anyone to come back home. His arms are always ready and open wide to receive His son/daughter. And here is the best part, there is no working to get back to anything! You are immediately restored! Isn't our God merciful, loving and kind? I rejoice with the angels and all of Heaven for anyone who decides to come home! Welcome back my brother/sister.

Prayer: Father Thank You! Thank You so much that You have provided a way for us to come home. We have all sinned and fallen short of Your glory but because of the God-Man Jesus Christ, You have torn the veil and left an open invitation back to the table of Your grace. I bless You, Father for my brother/sister who has made the decision to rededicate their lives to You. Today as we stand before Your presence, we declare with our mouths that we believe with our hearts that You have restored us today. We break the covenant that we have made with hell in our hour of rebellion and we say to You, Father that here we are to stay. Forgive us of the sin the beset us and caused us to leave the safety of Your love. Welcome us home according to the magnitude of Your loving-kindness. We thank You again Father, for Your mercy and for Your great love! In Jesus' name we pray, amen.

Day 99- **Prayer of Salvation**

Out of all the prayers that have been prayed in this book and the prayers that will be prayed in your life this is one of the utmost importance. And if you have never prayed this prayer, none of this really matters until you do! This brings you into covenant with Yahweh, the one who keeps covenants and gives you access to all of His promises. It is the prayer that brings us before our loving God and begins a life long friendship with Him and makes Jesus the Lord over our lives. If you are praying this prayer for the first time, congratulations on making the best decision in your life. If you leading someone to Christ, then even better! I do not claim there is any one way to lead someone or to pray the prayer of salvation. However here is the scriptural basis for this prayer.

Romans 10:9-10 says " *That if you confess with your mouth the Lord Jesus and believe in your heart that God has raised Him from the dead, you will be saved. For with the heart one believes unto righteousness, and with the mouth confession is made unto salvation.*"

If you or someone you know has come to the decision to make Jesus the Lord of their life, pray this prayer with them.

Prayer: Jesus, today I have come to a decision in my heart that I rather not live life without You. I realized that I have sinned and come short of Your glory. I stand in need of Your salvation. I confess that You are the Son of the living God and that He has raised You from the dead. I believe this with my whole heart. And because of that testimony, I make You the Lord over my life for the rest of my life! Congratulations on your decision!!!!!

Day 100

We are here! We have come to the end of the campaign. We did it! And I firmly believe that God has done it! Everything that your heart has petitioned Him for, it is done. As a full declaration of faith, declare it to be so! It is my sincerest hope that this campaign has not only encouraged you but perhaps has even elevated your faith and has taken your prayer and worship life to the next level. Besides, with your newly healed body, mind and soul, you are going to need some of the tools to finish the mandate and purposes that God has placed on your life. How exciting? I pray nothing but the Lord's best in your life for the rest of your life! As I bring this book to a close, I want to pray for you Mr/Ms/Mrs. Reader as to send you on your way back into the ranks as one who has been visited by the Great Physician and is ready to recover all!

Prayer: Father, we thank you! With exuberance in our hearts we eagerly await the confirmed word of Your healing and deliverance. Thank You, God for the written word that imparts life into us. As the reader sits and meditates on Your word, it brings success to every failing and dying situation. At the entrance of Your word, there is light. It illuminates the darkest areas of our mind and drives out every thought that is contrary to what you have spoken. Thank You, Lord that it is Your will to heal Your people. And as Your healing settles upon their bodies and mind, it is my prayer that they will run to tell the testimony of Jesus and His healing graces. Holy

Spirit, I ask that You would be their companion in the realest way. Show them the truth of the Father and the truth of who they are in Christ. We understand that this healing is so that the Glory of God may be made manifest in the earth and that the knowledge of His glory will cover the earth as the waters cover the sea. Get the glory out of their lives, Lord Jesus. Manifest yourself through them to everyone that they encounter. You said that "And I, if I am lifted up from the earth, I'll draw all men unto myself." (John 12:32) We say to You, Lord "Be lifted up! And Be thou Glorified through us." And never shall we give Your glory to another. Never shall we give your glory to modern medicine or the philosophies of man. But all glory and honor is due your righteous and holy name. And it is in the powerful, saving, healing and delivering name of Jesus I pray, Amen.